D0746457

DIVERSITY PARTNERSHIP TIPS FOR WHITE MEN:
A SKILLS-BUILDING FIELD GUIDE

By: Bill Proudman, Michael Welp and Jo Ann Morris

WMFDP, LLC

WMFDP, LLC
PO Box 12436
Portland, OR 97212
(503) 281-5585

Order books at www.wmfdp.com

ISBN 0-9754192-1-8
Library of Congress Control Number: 2004107089

TESTIMONIALS

"This very practical and action-oriented field guide is written for the white male interested in forging effective diversity partnerships. The tips and reflective questions will help you accelerate the pace of change relative to diversity in your life and organization."

Michael Kennedy
President, Transportation Business Group, CH2M HILL

"This guide is direct, clear, easy to read, engaging and development/action oriented. It healthfully addresses matters critical and beneficial for everyone involved in diversity work."

Robert Hayles, Ph.D.
Coauthor of *The Diversity Directive* and former Chair of the Board of Directors for ASTD (American Society for Training & Development)

"Proudman, Welp, and Morris are pioneers in defining the effects of white male culture on leadership and business results. These field guides, based on the proven principles of their extensive research and work in organizations, place in the hands of leaders a practical tool that will immediately impact the people and organizations using them."

Lars Houmann
Executive Vice President and Chief Operating Officer, Florida Hospital

"This field guide offers a nonthreatening, enlightening challenge to action that gives white males the keys to creating more inclusive, satisfying and effective relationships across lines of difference. Blame, guilt and defensiveness are not part of this process. Clear information, guidelines and examples for real change are. This is a powerful addition to the resources for healthy, practical and effective diversity management."

Anita Rowe
Partner in Gardenswartz & Rowe and coauthor, *Managing Diversity: A Complete Desk Reference and Planning Guide*

TESTIMONIALS

"These field guides on Partnership in Diversity address the chasm separating millions of white men from their natural allies in creating inclusive relationships, groups, organizations, and communities. They point the way with clear examples and models that will inform and promote deep understanding and collaboration in the pursuit of social justice."

Charlie Seashore and Edie Seashore
Recipients of the Lifetime Achievement Awards of the Organization Development Network

"Progress is made when we ask the other group what they want. This guide grows out of years of workshops and discussions with white men. It offers critical insights into what white men will need to be partners in creating more diverse and inclusive organizations."

Fred Miller and Judith Katz
Kaleel Jamison Consulting Group, Inc., and coauthors of *The Inclusion Breakthrough*

CONTENTS

ACKNOWLEDGMENTS

Many people helped us in the creation of this field guide. Foremost we thank our clients, whose partnership has helped us shape and evolve our ideas. Our appreciation also goes to our associates, who share our passion, support our ongoing growth and help us proudly serve our clients. Special thanks to our business partner Tim McNichol who challenged and supported the evolution of our work. Thanks also to Jim Barber, Jeff Schmidt, Mike Kennedy, and Mark Chesler for reviewing this text and providing valuable feedback.

INTRODUCTION TO THE WMFDP FIELD GUIDE SERIES

White Men as Full Diversity Partners® (WMFDP, LLC) is a company driven by a desire to change the way diversity is practiced in the United States. We believe that building effective diversity partnerships creates critical leadership skills that have often been absent from most organizations' leadership development and diversity initiatives. We believe diversity partnerships leverage leadership skills and can be developed throughout an organization.

We are pursuing three goals in the establishment of diversity partnerships and inclusive organizations:

1] The first goal is the automatic inclusion of white men and their diversity rather than including everyone else but white men.

2] The second is the inclusion of work that women and men of color, and white women are invited to do to examine how their assumptions, interactions, and experiences influence their diversity partnerships with white men as well as their interactions with each other.

3] The third is the ability of leaders to see and act on the symbiotic relationship between leadership skill development and the creation of diversity partnerships. Linking leadership and diversity partnerships on a daily basis can transform mindsets and build skills. The results are courageous actions that benefit people and the goals of their organizations.

It doesn't matter to us what position you hold. What does matter is that all of us have work to do and a role to play in changing the way diversity is practiced and valued.

This field guide for white men is a companion to another guide for white women, and men and women of color, which outlines the work they need to do to create break-through diversity partnerships, and a third field guide which focuses on the eight critical leadership skills developed through diversity partnership work. This guide was written to support you. In order to benefit, you will need to take action: read, reflect on the questions, experiment with the activities, and apply the insights to your work and life. Use this guide to increase your understanding of diversity, your leadership ability, and your diversity partnership skills. Your actions today and tomorrow are what count.

The partners and associates of WMFDP, LLC are grateful for our clients' courageous actions and persistence in doing the work that creates diversity partnerships and makes inclusive organizations a reality.

WHO SHOULD USE THIS FIELD GUIDE?

This field guide focuses on the practice and refinement of diversity partnership skills. It is written in a conversational tone and speaks directly to you the reader. Anyone who wants to learn more about partnerships and what it takes to build and sustain them can use and benefit from this field guide. Specifically, the guide is intended for:
- Business leaders and managers
- Diversity councils and employee networks
- Individuals and groups in for-profit and non-profit organizations
- Professors and their students

How to Use This Field Guide

This is a "take-action" field guide. It is designed for you to use interactively – at work, in your community and your personal life. No field guide works in the same way for any two people, so we have included a variety of ways to look at the topics explored in the field guide.

Historically, white women and people of color have done almost all of the work of educating white men on diversity issues. Transforming this dynamic – such that white men, white women, and women and men of color partner together effectively – is not effortless, but it is possible. Pursuing diversity partnership work requires new ways of thinking and new behaviors. All of the field guides were written to help you do the work; the choice is yours.

The first half of this field guide introduces tips, skill descriptions and reflective questions to help you apply the skills described.

The second section provides activities to further develop these skills. Some of the activities can be done individually, while others are suggested for group work. Work with each tip, or strategy, and use the field guide to push yourself further out onto your learning edge.

While these guides primarily address issues related to race and gender, many of the tips and questions are applicable to other kinds of difference; for example, sexual orientation, age and economic background. These diversity partnerships are also key to organizational health and business success.

Some helpful suggestions when using this field guide:

1] The intent of the field guide is to help you become more conscious and competent in the development and application of diversity partnership skills. It takes perseverance and practice. Don't expect perfection or immediate results.

2] Work alone and with others. Find ways to work with colleagues and/or friends. This work is about partnership and reflection. You might begin with solo reflection by answering questions you find in the field guide. Your next step might be to ask a colleague or friend to work with you. Have them act as a coach or mentor, someone to talk through how you are putting into action the tip or skill you chose.

3] Don't attempt to read through the field guide cover to cover. Take it one small chunk at a time. Read through each tip and work the one that appeals to you the most. Work with one reflective question at a time.

4] Take notes. Notice what is easy and makes sense and where you become confused and/or resistant. Use your coach to talk through those spots and seek learning that brings *immediate* relevancy to your diversity partnership efforts at work.

5] Acknowledge and celebrate each small step forward in strengthening your partnership skills practice. If you feel stuck in one spot, move onto another tip or reflective question.

6] This field guide is an entry into a variety of partnership strategies, not an exhaustive list. Approach the study of diversity partnership the way an anthropologist would go on a dig. Look at things from different angles. Be curious. Ask questions. Write your own reflective questions. Suspend judgment.

As you deepen your practice of diversity partnership we invite you to tell us what you are learning. Share reflective questions that you created by using this field guide. Your insights will help direct subsequent revisions of the guide. Email your comments and additions to **fieldguides@wmfdp.com**

Based on our experiences with a wide range of clients, if you commit to this skill-building adventure, you'll discover more choices in how you relate to and interact with others. You will become more aware of how you are developing and using your skills and resources in new ways. You will also be more equipped to use them in creating effective and satisfying partnerships built on shared understanding, whether at work or at home.

ABOUT THE "WHAT SKILLS YOU MIGHT SEE" SECTION

We have added a story for each of the 10 tips listed in this field guide. These stories are actual events that our clients have shared with us. The stories illustrate how each person demonstrated partnership skills.

We have talked to numerous white women, and men and women of color, who have sometimes questioned the authenticity of their white male colleagues' commitment to diversity. Given how diversity has traditionally been practiced, it makes sense that many white women, men and women of color and other white men have few examples of white men authentically engaged in corporate diversity efforts.

A NOTE ABOUT OUR HISTORY

In 1996, we embarked on a novel experiment that attempted to bring groups of white men together to examine how issues about race, gender and sexual orientation affected them and their partnerships with other white men as well as with white women, and men and women of color. Over time, we have had the privilege of working with hundreds of white men, white women, and men and women of color. Their tenacity and courage to re-examine their diversity partnerships give us hope that we can collectively transform how diversity is practiced for optimal business results. The business results are grounded in how white men, white women, and men and women of color communicate and work effectively together.

Following are some quotes from white men who have participated in our 3½-day "White Men's Caucus" Learning Labs.

"Over 10 years ago I began the diversity journey, full of energy and wanting to do what's right. Along the way I learned to become resentful and angry about the process and progress women, people of color and gay/lesbian groups were going through. It felt like everything I did was wrong and I was a target of their anger, fear, and hostility. As a result, my personal progress became "frozen" – if anything you do is wrong, the only right thing to do was nothing. I have finally begun to explore how I really felt about diversity and other groups in the company of others like myself.

"As a result I believe I am beginning to 'get it.' What women, people of color and homo/bisexuals need for me to do is to create the space for them to be themselves, with their unique and collective strengths and weaknesses, to make life better for all of us."

"I now know that I was born into something with no choice, trained to not show emotion or concern for things outside my "box," but also knowing I can make a difference even with just starting with me and moving forward one step at a time."

"I am more aware now as a white male of the daunting task and amount of work before us all on issues of inclusivity. However, I am deeply moved and heartened by the fact that I now realize that I have many more potential allies (white males) in carrying forward this work than I thought."

"White men are a key part of my family that I have never acknowledged. I have been ashamed of you and refused to take part in your activities or take responsibility for our actions. I am determined to remedy this at a personal level, using our common sources of strength to work change in myself and my gender/class."

"I have to say that this caucus has been the most personally rewarding experience of my life. Never before have I sat down with other men (or in fact anyone) and tackled such difficult issues in such a productive way. I have a level of respect and connection to these individuals that I never felt was possible."

"I have always said, 'I treat everyone the same' and 'I treat everyone as equals.' I discovered what I really meant was that I hold myself to certain standards, standards that are tied to and influenced by white male culture in America, and furthermore I hold you to those same standards. Assimilate or fail."

"I found a culture (white male culture) that contained elements that I admire and despise. This culture is ours to keep or change. We suffer because of the way the culture defines us and others suffer because of the way we define them. Diversity is not about moving over or giving up power or law. It is about learning and using the best all have to offer. Diversity is not about dividing a limited resource but expanding resources. We have the power and responsibility to begin to define a new culture that does not exclude but respectfully values all people."

"Supporting diversity isn't about white men losing anything. It's about being part of a group that can learn and stumble through issues together. White men need to talk about diversity and the feelings it generates. I also know that it's all right to be in the place that I am right now with my journey, and that being confused at times is very natural."

KNOW THAT YOU ARE PERCEIVED AS BOTH A MEMBER OF THE WHITE MALE GROUP AND AS AN INDIVIDUAL.

As white men, most of us perceive ourselves as individuals. We may see women as a group and people of color in their various groups, but when it comes to us, we don't perceive ourselves as part of a white male group. We tend to think of ourselves primarily as individuals. In part, this difference is a reflection of our American white male culture.* It emphasizes rugged individualism. While we see ourselves as individuals, others we work with will likely see us as part of a group of white men, *and* as individuals. When others group us, we do not lose our individuality. It is not an "either/or." It is a paradox** that we are both individuals *and* part of a white male group.

---

* See appendix for more on European-American or American white male culture.
** See appendix for more on paradoxes of diversity for white men.

Understanding diversity, and working with and across diversity, requires accepting complexity. We are each part of other groups, too; groups related to our age, class, religion, physical and mental ability, and other dimensions.

What is it about being a white male that can make this paradox troublesome? Bottom line: White men have a different experience of the world due to being in this group. We generally don't have to experience things in the world that other groups experience. Our general unawareness of that difference is what causes others to say, "You just don't get it." Until we begin to look at what it means to be white and male, and separate that out from what it means to be human and/or American, we won't get it. And not only will we not know, we won't know that we don't know.

As you learn about what it means to be white and male, you will develop the skills to be able to distinguish whether a person is talking to you as an individual and/or as a member of the white male group. Making the distinction between the two reduces the possibility that you will take what is said personally. Every comment white women, or men or women of color make about white men is not necessarily about you specifically. Explore how this perception influences communication and understanding between you and your colleagues.

WHAT SKILLS YOU MIGHT SEE

Keith, the new leader of a senior team, missed a staff meeting due to an out-of-office engagement. At the meeting there had been an incident where the team's two women members had finally shared their pent-up frustration about the difficulties they face every day as women in a male-dominated environment. Among other things they shared how they experienced their ideas being frequently discounted by men in meetings.

Two of the white men on the team had felt personally attacked by the women's comments and felt they were being blamed because they were white and male.

Keith used his normal one-on-one meetings with his team to ask the men to consider how seeing oneself as an individual, most or all of the time, might impact or affect what they hear, especially when other folks are talking about their experiences with white men. Knowing that both men have daughters in their mid-twenties, Keith also invited them to think about what this work environment might be like for their daughters. Keith mostly listened to the men, acknowledging what they were saying.

Keith blocked out time at the next staff meeting to discuss the event. During that session, Keith talked at length about his desire for this team to engage in more difficult conversations. The goal would be to strengthen their ability to work effectively together and to understand differences so they can benefit from the differences.

He requested team members:
- *Share some of what they experienced from the conversation at the meeting.*
- *Talk about how they perceived the intent of what others had said.*
- *Examine the gap between the intent of what each person said in the previous meeting and how it had impacted other team members.*
- *Agree to examine this issue further.*
- *Consider how to move forward.*

Through this incident and the conversation that followed, team members gradually built the skills to negotiate difficult conversations, and the white men learned to see themselves as both individuals and members of a white male group. The team drew closer and more candid and effective in future discussions.

Resulting Changes:
- *Increased capacity by senior leaders to negotiate difficult conversations.*
- *Modeling to others that such conversations strengthen decision making.*
- *Greater ability to simultaneously see oneself as both an individual and a member of a group.*
- *Less defensiveness by white men when hearing women discuss the challenges they face.*

REFLECTIVE QUESTIONS:

1] What do I know about what it means to me to be white and male at my place of work? How might this be different from being a person at work who is not white and/or male?

_____

_____

_____

_____

_____

_____

_____

_____

_____

_____

2] What do I generally share in common with other white men that I may not be fully aware of? How might those who are not white and male perceive me as a member of the white male group?

_____

_____

_____

_____

_____

_____

_____

_____

_____

_____

3] What might be the indicators that someone is talking to me as a member of the white male group as opposed to me as an individual human?

_____

_____

_____

_____

_____

_____

_____

_____

4] Many white men say, "I never thought of myself as a member of the white male group." What does it mean for me to begin seeing this as an aspect of who I am? What judgments or reactions come up for me?

_____

_____

_____

_____

_____

_____

_____

_____

5] What might I be afraid of losing by acknowledging who I am as a white man?

_____

_____

_____

_____

_____

_____

_____

REALIZE THE LEARNING NEVER ENDS — CULTIVATE AN APPETITE FOR NEW LEARNING.

It seems that the more we learn about diversity the more we realize how much we still don't know. This can feel overwhelming, especially when we are used to learning something, mastering it and, therefore, feeling like we've 'got it wired'. We check it off our list and move on.

Not so with diversity: the learning never ends. Yet we want to know what the diversity "rules" are. "Just tell me what the rules are and I'll follow them." For example, "What name should I call 'them' and their group?" We can be frustrated that "they" don't all want to be called the same name (e.g. African-American or Black, Latinos or Hispanic). This is a good example of how we see others as a group and expect them to each want the same thing. Remember in the last tip how we want to be seen as individuals? Others are individuals too. There are no simple rules – so continuous learning is a requirement in this arena.

The need to be right is one thing that can block learning. You don't take in others' experiences very well when you are busy defending your viewpoint. Know that it is less about your view being wrong and more that your view is an incomplete picture of the whole. Act on what you know, while also seeking insight and a broader perspective through the eyes and voices of others. Stay in touch with both your wisdom and your humility. In doing so, others will be able to experience you as human and imperfect. They will support your learning and feel more comfortable learning and working with you.

WHAT SKILLS YOU MIGHT SEE

Frank, a senior engineer in a consulting firm, was initially surprised, shocked and even disbelieving of stories he heard from women engineers about difficulties they faced at work on a daily basis. Instead of discounting the women or giving examples of men having some of the same experiences (as a way to justify that there is no difference regarding gender), Frank worked to deepen his partnerships with a few senior women with whom he had already built trust. He asked questions of their everyday work experiences and for examples where they felt ignored or discounted simply because they were women.

Over time, Frank learned to observe for himself some of the micro-inequities that women face daily in his work environment. Now when he notices these inequities, he points them out to other men and women colleagues and reminds himself that the inequities are real and need to be addressed. All the individuals on his team now have a greater voice at the table, and contribute more fully to business results.

Resulting Changes:
– *Strengthened skill with inquiring about another's perceptions.*
– *Increased ability to perceive and address workplace problems.*
– *Willingness to use curiosity as a valuable tool instead of jumping immediately to problem solving.*

REFLECTIVE QUESTIONS:

1] When was the last time I learned something because I wanted to? What was it?

_____

_____

_____

_____

_____

_____

_____

2] How might my childhood learning experiences about others be helping or hindering my ability to be an effective diversity partner today?

_____

_____

_____

_____

_____

_____

3] How does making my intentions clear to others support learning, communication, and my ability to be an effective leader and diversity partner?

_____

_____

_____

_____

_____

_____

_____

4] What have I chosen to say to my diversity partners but decided not to, and why? If I were to say it, what do I imagine might happen to that partnership?

_____

_____

_____

_____

_____

_____

_____

5] What do I already feel I "know" about diversity partnerships? How might this "knowing" block my continued learning?

_____

_____

_____

_____

_____

_____

_____

6] How does it feel as a leader to admit I don't know, or am at a loss when it comes to some issues around diversity? How does this impact my credibility?

_____

_____

_____

_____

_____

_____

IT'S NOT YOUR FAULT AND YOU ARE RESPONSIBLE.

Don't apologize for things you have not done. Instead, seek to understand how you participate in maintaining systems that hurt many people and continue to benefit you and your group. Don't allow your receipt of benefits as a member of the white male group to mute your voice or prompt you to respond from a place of guilt. Guilt can be an interesting place to visit, but it's not a helpful place to stay. Guilt can subtly keep you focused on your perception of your innocence. When you are stuck in guilt it can deter you from learning about other people's experiences. It can also deter you from recognizing more fully how you unintentionally contribute in the present to inequality in the workplace and from acting to address the issues you see.

Most white men value equality deeply and genuinely. In our worldview we often see ourselves as treating everyone the same. And in our not knowing what we don't know, our definition of "sameness" is based on a white male norm. If we have not looked at what it means to be white and male, we generally equate it with what it means to be a good human and/or American. We often treat everyone the same with an unknown assumption that one should first act like a white male. *I will treat you the same based on a set of conditions. As long as you hold down your emotion, are able to 'go it alone' without asking for much help, are into action (over too much reflection), and allow a sharp linear sense of time to drive your life, then I will be willing to treat you the same.* Transcend the blame conversation so you can study what is really going on in the here and now.

WHAT SKILLS YOU MIGHT SEE

Brian, a white male foreman in a manufacturing operation, was acutely aware that one line employee, Ron, an African-American, had a reputation with white employees for turning every conversation into a race issue. In this predominantly white company, Ron was regarded as an angry man who played the race card at just about every opportunity. He had no close white friends and was largely relegated to talking with a small number of African-American employees.

Ron was passionate about most things in life and his passion was often misinterpreted as anger by whites. This reaction just made Ron more passionate and determined. Over time, Ron began to display more outbursts of frustration. These often elicited more response from whites, which reinforced Ron's suspicions that most whites were clueless about the effects of race.

Ron continued to speak his mind. He talked a lot about how race affected his every move. He rarely had a positive work relationship with any white man and viewed most white men as clueless to the plight of African-Americans.

Brian, after participating in a White Men as Full Diversity Partners diversity learning lab, decided to engage Ron in a series of conversations to hear more about how racism had impacted Ron's life and his view of the world. His purpose was to "listen to understand" Ron. He made this effort in a sincere desire to build a partnership with Ron, who was very technically talented, but isolated and misunderstood at the plant.

In the early going, Ron was suspicious of Brian's intentions, wondering why all of a sudden a white guy was interested in this topic. During the first few months of Brian's overtures, Ron vigorously challenged and questioned Brian's intent.

Brian was not deterred. After a few months of occasional conversations at work and in the lunchroom, Brian and Ron were still talking. It wasn't easy, but both men were learning from each other. Early on, Brian told Ron that he did not want Ron to "tone it down" (something Ron often heard from whites). Brian further asked Ron to let him know if any of his actions or behaviors were offensive or inappropriate.

Brian further grappled with Ron's occasional request that Brian and other white men apologize for the actions of other white people. Brian made it clear to Ron that he was empathetic and wanted to better understand Ron's experience with racism, yet he let Ron know it was not helpful for him to apologize for things he had not done. He was shocked that Ron's life had been so difficult, and wondered how he might have reacted if he had faced much of what Ron experienced in his life.

Brian learned a lot from hearing Ron's story. He gained confidence in better separating someone else's struggles with race from feeling at fault or blame because he is white. Brian and Ron worked hard and, over time, began to build trust. They listened to understand without taking responsibility for the other's struggles.

Resulting Changes:

– *Strengthened ability to see and work with ambiguity.*

– *Deepened empathy of others' different realities.*

– *Strengthened work relationships so people felt more valued and heard.*

– *Willingness to hang in there during difficult conversations and not take on or accept unwarranted blame.*

REFLECTIVE QUESTIONS:

1] Why is maintaining my innocence so important? What do I gain by maintaining my innocence or ignorance?

_____

_____

_____

_____

_____

_____

_____

_____

_____

_____

_____

_____

2] When I put questions of guilt and innocence aside, what new questions emerge?

_____

_____

_____

_____

_____

_____

_____

_____

_____

_____

_____

3] How might my assumptions about blame or guilt silence me?

_____

_____

_____

_____

_____

_____

_____

_____

_____

_____

_____

_____

_____

4] What advice could I give peers about having effective but difficult conversations related to fault and responsibility? Do I apply that advice to my own difficult conversations?

_____

_____

_____

_____

_____

_____

_____

_____

_____

_____

_____

_____

WORK HARD TO BETTER UNDERSTAND SYSTEMIC PRIVILEGE.

The rugged individualism of our American white male culture prevents us from seeing ourselves as a group and from recognizing that we have a different experience in the world by being white, male, and (for some of us) heterosexual. Not only do we have a culture, but also our group membership affords us systemic privileges along several dimensions.

WHAT DO WE MEAN BY SYSTEMIC PRIVILEGE?

Systemic privilege is the web of unspoken, invisible benefits that come to a person by no virtue of their own. The benefits are made to look normal and hence, available to any person.

Being a recipient of systemic privilege based on skin color, gender or sexual orientation does not prevent straight white men from feeling mistreated or personally powerless in individual interactions. That said, not understanding how the benefits of systemic privilege impact day-to-day interactions can lead to an enormous barrier in effectively understanding, communicating and leading diverse organizations. To support our understanding of systemic privilege, here are some examples:

White Privilege:
1] I don't have to think about or worry about whether I got a job or promotion solely because of my race. Nor do I have to worry about whether my peers think this was the case.
2] My children's teacher won't make negative assumptions about the capabilities of my son or daughter based on his/her race.
3] I can express my opinion in public without putting my race on trial.

Male Privilege:
1] I seldom have to worry about my own safety when I go out walking or running at night. My women colleagues exert more effort monitoring their own safety.
2] I am rarely, if ever, judged based on the cleanliness and/or neatness of my house.
3] On the job, I am not judged by the attractiveness of my appearance.

Heterosexual Privilege:
1] I can have pictures of loved ones on my desk and not have to worry about what people will think.
2] I can talk about what I did last weekend without having to edit what I say.
3] I will not be denied access to my partner's hospital bedside if there is a life-threatening illness or accident.

Privilege can be thought of as less about what you have and more about what you *don't have to deal with*. Being white, male and heterosexual, the ultimate privilege is to not have to think about those aspects of my identity. Because I rarely have to think about these dimensions of difference, another privilege related to diversity is that I can choose when and if I want to think about and address diversity issues. In today's environment of political correctness, I may choose to play it safe, and not speak out and engage in how issues of diversity are influencing business outcomes and/or how privilege is distributed. Unfortunately, my inaction ultimately reinforces the inequality in place both at work and in the world because the status quo has its own momentum. By my inaction, I reinforce the status quo.

My reaction to the concept of affirmative action is likely based on my current perceptions of whether the 'playing field' is level or not. If I feel the playing field is level, I will see affirmative action as giving unfair advantage to some groups. If I feel the playing field is not level, I may see affirmative action as partly an attempt to level the playing field.

Do systemic privileges, such as the examples mentioned above, and the permeation of white male culture throughout the workplace serve as an invisible form of 'affirmative action' benefiting white men?

When white women, men and women of color, and GLBT groups share experiences of struggles related to the privileges described above, as white men we can easily invalidate or discredit their experiences, because they are not experienced by white men. Anyone whose reality is invalidated tends to get angry and frustrated, and may respond with "you don't get it."

Occasionally, a person of color or white woman may "play the race/gender card" and blame a situation on racism or sexism when this is not the case. When one person of color or woman plays the race/gender card like this, it reflects negatively on their colleagues of color or female colleagues because we (in seeing them as a group) might assume they all do that.

In reality, white men play the race/gender card more frequently, and rarely get called on it. We might say, or simply think, "so and so employee only got the job because of his/her race."

It is helpful to our partnerships with each other and with white women, and men and women of color, to hear how we frame our statements about issues of diversity. We may be surprised by the inadvertent messages we send out to others.

WHAT SKILLS YOU MIGHT SEE

Mike and Bob are two senior leaders who attended a White Men as Full Diversity Partners diversity session together. The session increased their awareness of white male privilege and its impact on the workplace. They continued to partner with each other and formed a white men's affinity network within their company. They have both learned to see how white male privilege shows up in the work place, and how it impacts white women, and men and women of color. They are simultaneously learning to view themselves as not guilty, or at fault, simply because they happen to be white and male. Instead, they are learning to recognize privilege and use it honorably to effect positive change in their company.

They continue to utilize their support network of other white men. They don't rely solely on women and people of color to interpret for them when they are confused or others misinterpret their efforts.

They recognize that fear and misunderstanding may occur when people attempt to examine the effect of systemic privilege in the workplace. They know they are in it for the long haul, and constantly work to understand their own self-interest in the company's ongoing diversity efforts. They focus on how those efforts impact the way they do business with each other internally and with their customers. Surprisingly, they feel more energized and powerful at work because of their newfound ability to bring up and sensibly discuss issues that they were previously ignorant of, or just did not see.

Resulting Changes:

– *Alignment of diversity policy (includes everyone) with practice.*
– *An increase in dialogue between white men, white women,*
  and men and women of color about the role white men must
  play in ongoing diversity efforts.
– *Less reliance on white women, and men and women of color,*
  to lead the diversity effort. All employees can have a stake
  in inclusion.

REFLECTIVE QUESTIONS:

1] What don't I know about the day-to-day interactions of my colleague's life that might be impacting our day-to-day partnership?
(Completing activity 1 may help you answer this question.)

_____

_____

_____

_____

_____

_____

_____

_____

_____

_____

_____

2] How might privilege (as defined previously) be impacting my interactions with others at work?

_____

_____

_____

_____

_____

_____

_____

_____

_____

_____

_____

_____

3] How would my work day differ if I had to constantly be aware of diversity issues for my advancement and success?

_____

_____

_____

_____

_____

_____

_____

_____

4] How can I learn to avoid invalidating another person's reality that is different from my own?

_____

_____

_____

_____

_____

_____

_____

5] In what ways can I stay open to another person's reality and to understanding him/her more fully, rather than judging him/her from my own frame of reference?

_____

_____

_____

_____

_____

_____

_____

EXPECT TO MAKE MISTAKES.

Expect some of your mistakes to disappoint or hurt others. Have the tenacity and courage to learn from your missteps. More important than what mistakes you make is how you respond to them. Will you stay on the path of learning, in the turbulence of uncertainty, and work through difficult conversations to the place of insight and learning? You have a history of success. Find it. Where in your life have you stuck it out in hard times? Do it again.

Don't be afraid to be vulnerable. Counter to the tough white male archetypes of the media, vulnerability is actually a strength. A leader who is strong without ever being vulnerable is not as powerful as a leader who is both strong and vulnerable. Vulnerability demonstrates a deeper courage and authenticity, and moves the hearts and minds of others. It also makes it safer for others to be authentic and open to learning.

Balance your "mistakes" by noticing and celebrating your strides forward. Expect to learn more and do better. Be kind to yourself along the way. Learning requires challenge and support; build both into your relationships with others. That means you receive both support and challenge from others and you give it to them. To support a colleague, without ever challenging him or her (from a place of compassion), limits the potential learning that can stem from diversity partnerships.

WHAT SKILLS YOU MIGHT SEE

Martha, a female colleague with less seniority, confronted John, a foreman at a manufacturing plant, during a meeting. Martha told him that his behavior toward her, from more than a year ago, had been hurtful and was as yet unresolved. It had taken Martha more than a year to gain the nerve to confront John with the impact of his actions. He first responded by apologizing and telling her that it would never happen again. Over the next couple of days he continued to explore with Martha the impact of his previous behavior and stayed open to listening to understand her experience. He initiated more conversations with Martha and began to see his mistake as an opportunity to grow, and the confrontation by Martha as a gift to his learning.

This new behavior on John's part was initially difficult for him because he was uncomfortable knowing that his lack of awareness about his actions had been hurtful to Martha. He was also embarrassed that he had never realized this. With the support of the other men and women from his organization, he received ongoing coaching. He was able to look at how his actions had impacted Martha without beating himself up.

John initially had a knee-jerk desire to quickly apologize and move on, without understanding in more detail how his actions and behavior were hurtful. The support and coaching he got from his colleagues to hang in there, not fix it, and just listen, ultimately assisted John and Martha in deepening their partnership and forging a new bond of trust and understanding. As her anger diminished, Martha was able to hear John. She experienced her dialogue with him as validation. John left with new insights into listening and looking more carefully at the connection between his intent and the impact of his behavior.

Resulting Changes:
– *Increased productivity from those involved*
  because all felt heard and valued.
– *Strengthened work relationships leading*
  to increased productivity.
– *Increased willingness to negotiate future*
  difficult conversations.

REFLECTIVE QUESTIONS:

1] What might I do after "getting my hand slapped," other than saying "I am damned if I do and damned if I don't?"

_____

_____

_____

_____

_____

_____

_____

_____

_____

_____

_____

2] When I am feeling frozen or stuck in a diversity partnership, what behaviors/actions of others can help me get unstuck? What can I do to move forward?

_____

_____

_____

_____

_____

_____

_____

_____

_____

_____

REFLECTIVE QUESTIONS *Continued*

3] When I talk to other white men about diversity issues, what do I say and what
    don't I say? Why is that? What is the cost or impact to me of either choice?

_____

_____

_____

_____

_____

_____

_____

_____

_____

_____

_____

4] How do I know that my diversity partners understand my intentions?

_____

_____

_____

_____

_____

_____

_____

_____

_____

_____

_____

_____

5] How am I conscious of the distinction between when I am observing behavior, and when I am making interpretations or excuses for that behavior?

_____

_____

_____

_____

_____

_____

_____

_____

_____

_____

_____

6] How would others describe my ability to be both strong and vulnerable?

_____

_____

_____

_____

_____

_____

_____

_____

_____

_____

_____

BE IN IT FOR THE LONG HAUL.

Learning about diversity is a long-term process. There is no quick fix. Each insight often brings more questions. Learn to become more comfortable with the confusion that often accompanies the understanding of diversity and its dynamics at work. Learn to embrace the ambiguity that is present in the complexity of diversity at work. Often our frustration around diversity is caused in part by our attempts to oversimplify the issues around diversity. We want to go back to "just tell me what the rules are, and I'll follow them."

Tolerating ambiguity is a muscle to develop. It is a muscle needed by leaders today to cope with the uncertainties and changing demands of today's business environment. Let your engagement in diversity partnerships hone this important skill.

WHAT SKILLS YOU MIGHT SEE

Mark and Ed, two white male colleagues who have worked side by side for more than 20 years in a large accounting firm, initially came to a White Men as Full Diversity Partners diversity learning session seeking a quick fix to their diversity dilemmas. They were convinced that if they were just told the answers, then they could move past the diversity paralysis that seemed to envelope them and their colleagues.

Instead they came away from the session convinced that the confusion they and others felt served an important purpose. Over time they became aware that the confusion was actually an invitation to deepen the dialogue of understanding and curiosity available to them with white women, men and women of color, and other white men.

Their friendship helped keep that learning alive. Five years after that session, they remain committed to their learning as full diversity partners. They have developed a partnership team of white women, and men and women of color, that meets regularly over lunch to share learnings, musings and other dilemmas.

They and their colleagues model life-long learning that feeds their curiosity. They frequently admit that they are more confused on some issues of difference than when they first started; yet the confusion has not compromised their strengthened ability to take action and make a difference in their company's continuing diversity efforts.

Resulting Changes:
– *More resilience and skill in managing the continual
  changes in the business.*
– *Skill to be more proactive rather than reactive.*
– *Less lost time because of fear and resistance to change.*

REFLECTIVE QUESTIONS:

1] Why do I bother to be a full diversity partner? What do I have to gain?

_____

_____

_____

_____

_____

_____

_____

2] What do I know now about diversity and partnership that I didn't know months or years ago?

_____

_____

_____

_____

_____

_____

3] What lessons or insights have I learned from people who are different from me? How do those lessons impact me today?

_____

_____

_____

_____

_____

_____

_____

_____

4] What do my white male colleagues say and do to represent their willingness to be my diversity partners? What do white women, and men and women of color I work with, say or do to represent their willingness to be my diversity partners? Which of their actions and behaviors surprised me at first?

_____

_____

_____

_____

_____

_____

_____

_____

5] When given the opportunity to "deepen the dialogue of understanding," what do I do?

_____

_____

_____

_____

_____

_____

6] How does my need for clarity and answers mask the complexity inherent in diversity issues?

_____

_____

_____

_____

_____

_____

_____

YOU HAVE MORE TO GAIN FROM DIVERSITY
THAN YOU EVER IMAGINED.

D iversity usually focuses on everyone but white men. For example: With gender, the focus in on women. With race, the focus is on people of color. With sexual orientation, the focus is on gay, lesbian, bisexual, and transgendered men and women. This list goes on for other dimensions of diversity. There are several unintended consequences of this dynamic.

First, as heterosexual white men we don't think diversity is about us. We think it is about helping "those people with their issues." Second, our involvement in diversity efforts, while sincere, is still directed toward supporting others. Because the focus is on everyone else, we never look at what it means to be white, male and heterosexual. When the focus is broadened, white men start to discover some of the ways we experience the world differently related to these dimensions. White men also can come to realize we have a culture. It is not a "bad" culture. Cultures are not good or bad, but all cultures have upsides and downsides.

Being white and male means that we rarely have to leave our culture. The downside of this privilege is that we have the least awareness of our own culture. We are like the fish who is unaware of the water it is swimming in until it has to leave it. White women, men and women of color, and others go home and leave the white male culture permeating most workplaces and may say, "Thank goodness I can be myself." Since we never leave our culture, we just assume it is universal reality and it is the same as being a good human being or a good American. By engaging other cultures, we can paradoxically learn more about our own culture and who we are. Awareness of our culture gives us more choice as to how much to stay within the boundaries of that culture. Maybe we don't want to define all of our identity by what we do. (Especially if we are about to retire and/or lose our jobs.) Perhaps we want to step out of the rugged individualism and stop and ask for help or directions when we are lost. Maybe we don't want to live our lives 24/7 by such a strong linear concept of time. Loosening up the box of white male culture can give us new gifts, including deeper, more satisfying relationships with other white men. We discover that there is more than one way to be a white man.

Seek to deepen your understanding of your self-interest and how it is connected to your journey as a diversity partner. Your diversity learning journey may ultimately lead to new insights and discoveries, including a deeper understanding of self, a deeper sense of personal freedom to be more fully who you are, and more satisfying relationships with others. Continue to study your confusion until you find clarity about what is at stake for you in diversity.

WHAT SKILLS YOU MIGHT SEE

Over a three-year period more than 120 white men from a large oil company attended a multi-day learning lab designed to assist white men in understanding the impact of white male culture and their stake in becoming full diversity partners. As a result of their learning, a number of these men started a white men's affinity network to deepen their diversity partnerships with white women, and men and women of color, as well as other white men.

These men recognized that many of their professional relationships had been severely impacted by their lack of awareness of how race and gender affected their work relationships and their workplace.

The group offered a "lunch and learn" session. A panel of white men talked about diversity and partnerships; they also discussed the need to deepen their partnerships with other white men rather than relying solely on white women, and men and women of color, for their learning and understanding of diversity.

Through the new affinity network, they were able to invite others to talk about the suspicions that some white women, men and women of color, and other white men had expressed about the purpose of a white men's affinity group.

Resulting Changes:
– *Corporate diversity words and actions are better aligned.*
  Diversity does indeed include everyone.
– *More active engagement by more parts of the workforce*
  to examine how issues of diversity impact all groups, not just some.
– *White men less dependent on white women, and men and women of*
  color, to be their exclusive teachers about diversity.

REFLECTIVE QUESTIONS:

1] As a white man, what do I personally have to gain from working towards a more inclusive work environment?

_____

_____

_____

_____

2] How would I describe my "enlightened self-interest" in doing this work with other white men? With white women, and men and women of color?

_____

_____

_____

_____

3] How would I justify taking the time and effort to pay attention to diversity issues in my workplace? To myself? To my manager?

_____

_____

_____

_____

4] What parts of myself do I hide from other white men that make my work life more difficult than it needs to be? What strengths have I used to effectively partner with other white men around issues of difference?

_____

_____

_____

_____

_____

_____

ENGAGE OTHERS TO BUCK THE SYSTEM.

White male culture has us "go it alone." Don't. Stand up to the stereotypical archetypes like John Wayne or the Marlboro Man. Seek out other white men to learn with and from. If you ask most white men where they learned about diversity, most everything comes from white women, and men and women of color, and other elements of diversity. Almost no learning comes from other white men. That is an enormous burden on everyone else to educate white men. Ask them if you don't believe it. Learn to see other white men as key to your continuing diversity learning, much the same way that you may currently view the role of white women, and men and women of color. It is easier to do this if you include within your view of diversity a need to fully understand what it means to be white and male, as well as heterosexual.

Many white men grew up with the rugged individual archetype leading us on. But there is something else at play here. If we, as white men, ask for help, show much vulnerability or emotion, or soften our toughness, we wonder "what will the other guys think of me?" Think back to the playground and imagine what the other boys would call you if you took these risks? It is almost certain that you'd be called a term associated with being a girl or being gay. And, growing up, we all really want to be accepted by our peers. So now we often take any part of ourselves that might be interpreted as "girlish" or gay and hide it, disown it, or perhaps even find it in someone else so we can keep the focus off ourselves. Our own homophobia is used as a weapon to lock us into a role of "acting like a man." Boys say to their moms, "My friends are watching, please don't hug me in front of school anymore." Jokes about corporate teams having group hugs tap into the same buried fear.

For white men to see and use each other as sources of learning and growth in our diversity leadership journey, we need to transcend our qualms about these archetypes and fears in order to be free to fully support and challenge each other. Our partnerships, built on deeper levels of support and challenge, will also reinvigorate our partnerships with white women and with men and women of color.

WHAT SKILLS YOU MIGHT SEE

Howard, one of only two African-American men in his organization, worked at a hydropower plant located in a rural area. One day, he shared with a group of white men at work an incident that he and his family had experienced the night before. A van marked with the name of a local business had driven past his house and someone in the van shouted the "N" word.

This event was the latest in a string of ongoing experiences Howard and his family routinely experienced living in a small, rural, and predominantly white town.

Colleagues at this hydro project were two years into a substantial culture change effort focused on valuing differences when this event occurred. With a predominantly white male workforce and white male management team, Howard had enough trust in his colleagues to share with them what he and his family had experienced.

Shaken and shocked, the group of mostly white men decided they needed to take action and deepen the dialogue in the community about difference and acceptance.

Thirty members of the organization drafted and signed a letter that was published in the local newspaper the following week, objecting to the behavior, and calling for a town meeting to examine the effect of race in the town. Over 80 people showed up at that initial event. This led to a series of meetings that eventually included the police chief, city manager, county commissioners and a number of business people.

From one single event came a commitment to deepen the understanding of race in that community. Howard had never experienced white people caring much about his experience and was moved to see the clear demonstration of partnership and a willingness to speak out. His partnerships with his colleagues deepened. Collectively, they had created an environment in which it was safe to take risks. As a result, they created a healthier, more productive work environment and served as leaders in the community.

Resulting Changes:
- *Increased willingness to be oneself at work leading to greater productivity.*
- *Increased sense of trust between colleagues.*
- *Increased sense of personal effectiveness from taking action and making a difference.*
- *White men raising issues of diversity without looking to white women, and men and women of color, to initiate or approve.*

REFLECTIVE QUESTIONS:

1] What have I learned about working with other white men to be an effective diversity partner?

_____

_____

_____

_____

_____

2] Which of my behaviors and actions render me less effective in my diversity partnerships with white men? Which behaviors and actions from other white men make them less effective with me as a full diversity partner?

_____

_____

_____

_____

_____

3] What keeps me from asking for help from other white men around issues of diversity?

_____

_____

_____

_____

_____

4] What commitments or agreements can I make with my non-white male colleagues to ensure I am not burdening them with being my educator around issues of diversity?

_____

_____

_____

_____

_____

LEARN HOW TO LISTEN...AGAIN.

White male culture socializes us to take action. We are doers and problem solvers. Don't believe us? How often have you heard from your spouse or significant other: "I don't want you to fix me or solve this, I just want you to listen and hear me." We have to learn that when we hear "a problem" it doesn't imply a need, responsibility, or request to fix it.

Most white men have also been trained that in conversation it is valuable to "win" by debating and arguing your point. The purpose of a conversation is to convey my point and convince others. We spend most of our time advocating our point and little time inquiring and hearing others' perspectives. We might interpret listening time as space to use to regroup for our next argument. This approach does not promote mutual understanding. Sometimes there is a winner and a loser, sometimes there is just frustration.

In contrast, the goal of a conversation for learning is mutual understanding. This means we can hear the other person's perspective so well that we can state their intent in our own words and they would say "yes, you get it." When white women, and men and women of color, have different experiences to share, this is the level of listening that we need to hold ourselves (and other white men) accountable to use. It isn't that what the other person is saying is right, so therefore, I must be wrong. It is simply two people with different perspectives, which together give a broader picture of the whole.

Rediscover your curiosity. Remember you don't have to fix everything and you can't fix what you don't understand. Recognize that being a member of an advantaged group may have shielded you from accurately hearing others and understanding their reality. Ask how others would like to be treated, rather than assuming you already know.

WHAT SKILLS YOU MIGHT SEE

Jason is a senior leader in his fifties. He has held a variety of management positions and is thought well of in the company. He has been there for almost 20 years so has seen the demographics of the employee population change over the years. Jason is the kind of guy who wants his walk to match his talk. He has worked with women for a good part of his career in engineering and has been a supporter of their contributions being recognized and rewarded. He has tried to help them without fixing things for them. His partnership tool kit looked pretty good. It was well organized and each tool had its place and purpose. He had it laid out just right, or so he thought, until he started wondering why there were so few women in senior levels. He wondered because his closest women colleagues had stopped talking about their experiences in the company or he had stopped listening.

He began to question some of his colleagues about why if he, and other white men, respected the women in the organization, that more women weren't moving up. He began to question his own responses when asked about a woman's fit for a particular assignment, whether she could handle the tough clients, did she really have the right stuff. He began to listen more closely to himself.

Jason sought out women he knew well and asked pointed questions about their perceptions of his behavior toward women at work. He wanted to know whether his actions toward them had ever blocked their rise in the company or affected their credibility and business results with clients. He asked them if they felt the same or different level of scrutiny as they took on more profit-and-loss responsibility.

Jason began to explore with other white men how gender had often limited who got in front of what clients – who got to make the sale by fixing the client's problem. His open dialogue with women colleagues, and the work he did with other white men with whom he felt safe, led him to a surprising discovery. He had assumed he respected women by trying to treat them "equally." He now understood many more things were operating and that he had to change his laid-back approach to progress. He realized he needed to rearrange and enlarge his partnership tool kit. What motivated him? He has daughters. When he visualized them in the positions of his women colleagues, he decided to make the respect he has for women show up differently, more overtly, in real-time, and less passively. He says he can't quite explain what happened but he knows he and the business are better off because something did change – in him.

Resulting Changes:
– *Deep listening starting with himself.*
– *Willingness to reexamine and challenge old or existing assumptions — his and others'.*
– *Willingness to ask questions and not just check off a box.*

REFLECTIVE QUESTIONS:

1] What is it that causes me to stop listening to others?

_____

_____

_____

_____

_____

2] How might I listen differently if I took a stance of inquiry when presented with another person's differing perspectives and beliefs?

_____

_____

_____

_____

_____

3] What can I do to get myself back to listening when I find I am not listening?

_____

_____

_____

_____

_____

4] What actions or behaviors from others invite me to listen? Which of those actions/ behaviors do I exhibit myself, to invite others to listen to me?

_____

_____

_____

_____

_____

_____

SPEAK OUT PUBLICLY ON DIVERSITY ISSUES.

Engage other white men in diversity issues, instead of leaving it to the people most directly impacted by workplace inequities. We must learn to challenge and support each other, and do it without immediately looking to white women, and men and women of color, for validation. We can demonstrate full partnership in the workplace by publicly engaging our white male colleagues. When white women, and men and women of color, see us engaged with each other on this topic, it can be a sign of hope for them. They no longer have to be the one to speak up in a meeting when they or their colleagues' contributions are ignored or discounted.

Recognize that speaking out publicly demonstrates your own learning – imperfections and all. You are countering our ultimate privilege, that we can choose to ignore diversity issues, by interrupting the status quo. Be part of the solution in creating a workplace that brings out the best in everyone. Organizations succeed when all people can bring their energy and uniqueness to work.

WHAT SKILLS YOU MIGHT SEE

Jeff, a member of a diversity council at a chemical manufacturing plant, is one of two heterosexual white men on the council. He edits the plant's monthly diversity newsletter and facilitates in-house diversity awareness sessions for the predominantly white male employees of the plant.

His key message is that "diversity is about all of us, including white men." He has learned through trial and error to both challenge and support white men from a place of compassion. What this looks like is that Jeff can compassionately confront other white men when their actions or behavior may hurt or offend him or other work colleagues. He is able to do this without using his rank or position in the organization as the motivator. He often uses his own learning and mistakes. He supports other men whose actions sometimes comes from a place of not knowing or realizing the impact of their actions on others.

Jeff has maintained the respect of his white male peers. His convictions about the benefits of diversity to all set an example for other white men about what a full diversity partner looks like. He routinely challenges white men to look at their statements and assumptions about others. He also models his own diversity learning journey and does not act from a position of being "better than" or "I know it and you don't."

Resulting Changes:
– *Freedom from thinking that one must have all the answers before one can act.*
– *Deepened understanding about how diversity is about white men.*
– *Learning to both challenge and support others simultaneously rather than assuming you must choose one at the expense of the other.*

REFLECTIVE QUESTIONS:

1] In what situations do I choose to be silent? What are the impacts of this choice on my diversity partnerships and me?

_____

_____

_____

_____

_____

_____

2] Where in my life have I said difficult things to others, and how did it deepen the partnership? How did it affect my influence on others?

_____

_____

_____

_____

_____

_____

3] How might I change my attitudes and behaviors towards other white men? How would I compassionately tell white men what I need from them to become a full diversity partner with me?

_____

_____

_____

_____

_____

_____

4] What might I do after "getting my hand slapped" other than saying, "I am damned if I do and damned if I don't?"

_____

_____

_____

_____

_____

_____

_____

_____

5] How can I speak up about an issue I observe without blaming or making another white man feel attacked by me?

_____

_____

_____

_____

_____

_____

6] How often do I look for support or appreciation from white women or people of color when I do take the risk to speak up? What is my motivation for speaking up?

_____

_____

_____

_____

_____

_____

ACTIVITIES

ACTIVITY 1

HERE WE GO AGAIN

ACTIVITY 2

NEXT TIME YOU TRAVEL

ACTIVITY 3

WHAT I DON'T HAVE TO THINK ABOUT

ACTIVITY 4

RULES OF THE ROAD

ACTIVITY 5

MISTAKE OF THE MONTH CLUB

ACTIVITIES FOR WHITE MEN TO BUILD PARTNERSHIP SKILLS

ACTIVITY 1

HERE WE GO AGAIN

GOAL:
To practice how to better negotiate the paradox of group/individual. Negotiating this means you simultaneously are able to see yourself both as an individual and as a member of the white male group. This activity is written for a group of white men although individuals can do it on their own.
Estimated Time: 1-2 hours

STEPS
1] Write down a comment or two you heard recently after which you felt pigeonholed as a member of THAT group; the white male group.

_____

_____

_____

_____

_____

_____

_____

2] Note your reaction at the time, regardless of whether you verbalized it or just kept it to yourself.

_____

_____

_____

_____

_____

_____

3] Now look at the comment without judgment and ask yourself the following:

a. What did you assume about the speaker's intention from the comment?

_____

_____

b. What question(s) might you have asked the speaker at the time to gain a clearer understanding of their intent?

_____

_____

c. How might you have heard the comment differently if you had assumed that the comment was not about you individually, but about that person's experience with white men collectively?

_____

_____

d. What might you have done in the moment to invite a deeper diversity partnership with the speaker?

_____

_____

e. What did you learn from observing or being a part of the interaction?

_____

_____

f. What is it that you most want the speaker to know about your individuality? Why is this important?

_____

_____

g. What is it the speaker most wanted you to know, that goes beyond seeing yourself as just an individual? Why was this important to him or her?

_____

_____

Variation: Sample Responses
These are approaches you might take with people who are unaware that they are seeing/treating you as a representative of the white male group:

1] "Help me to better understand the intent of what you just said. Is what you said specifically about me, or about your dealings with others who look like me?"

_____

_____

_____

_____

_____

2] "Tell me about some of your life experience/interactions with white men that make you believe their actions represent most white men."

_____

_____

_____

_____

3] Repeat back and validate as true for them what you heard them say. Do this without taking on blame that is not yours.

_____

_____

_____

_____

4] Ask them if they are interested in hearing your perspective about how you heard their statement as an individual AND also as a member of the white male group. Be open to hearing "no."

_____

_____

_____

_____

NEXT TIME YOU TRAVEL

GOAL:
To uncover the nuance of privilege, be it white or male privilege. Systemic privileges are the unspoken, unacknowledged benefits that come to a person through no virtue of their own, but are made to look normal and available to any person who wants them.
Estimated Time: 15-30 minutes

STEPS
1] Pick a public spot such as an airport, train station, expensive restaurant or "galleria" mall. You can do this process in any public place. This example uses an airport as the locale. Take on the role of cultural anthropologist and observe how different people are treated based on their "group membership."

_____

_____

_____

_____

_____

1] Take notes on your observations of the following:
a. Notice who is in the first class line and who is not.

_____

_____

_____

_____

_____

b. How would you describe the people standing in that line?

_____

_____

_____

_____

NEXT TIME YOU TRAVEL

c. Notice how people get treated differently at the ticket counter. Use obvious differences - men and women, older people, business-attired people, whites and people of color; differences in dress; language differences; adults with children, etc.

_____

_____

_____

_____

_____

_____

d. What groups are represented and not represented in the first class and regular coach lines?

_____

_____

_____

_____

_____

_____

e. How do you think being in these lines affects how they are treated and how they expect to be treated?

_____

_____

_____

_____

_____

_____

f. How do a person's dress, accent, physical appearance and personal hygiene habits impact the type of service they receive?

_____

_____

_____

_____

_____

g. Imagine the effect on the people involved if they receive this sort of service or treatment day after day. What expectations might they develop about how they move through life?

_____

_____

_____

_____

_____

Variations: Try this activity at a train station, high-end mall, or five-star restaurant. Pay attention to how the role of entitlement affects behaviors.

Try this activity in little bursts over time, such as every time you travel in airports. Notice patterns and trends. Develop your observation skills. Work to suspend judgment and initially just collect data.

WHAT I DON'T HAVE TO THINK ABOUT

GOAL:
To deeply examine the privileges we generally don't have to think about.
Estimated Time: 20-30 minutes

STEPS
1] Pick one aspect of difference to focus on: race, gender, religion, age, status/level within organization, sexual orientation, etc.

_____

_____

    Using that aspect of difference, create a list of things that people in that particular group have to contend with at work, that you don't even have to think about. For example, as a heterosexual I can put a picture of my partner on my desk without fear that another colleague at work will use that information to limit my future advancement opportunities, etc.

_____

_____

_____

_____

_____

_____

2] When looking at the list, ask yourself:
a. What would it mean to me if I had to deal with those challenges every day at work?

_____

_____

_____

_____

_____

_____

b. How much energy might I have to divert or invest, just to be seen as competent
    in the organization?

_____

_____

_____

_____

_____

_____

_____

c. What are the work implications for me of not knowing vs. being aware of
    the impact of this privilege differential?

_____

_____

_____

_____

_____

_____

_____

d. What might the cumulative impact be on me and others in our organization
    of not knowing that this differential exists every day for some employees?

_____

_____

_____

_____

_____

_____

_____

RULES OF THE ROAD

GOAL:

To make conscious the invisible, often unspoken norms that impact people's perception and people's contributions – their own and others'.

Estimated Time: 90-120 minutes

STEPS

Do this in a mixed group of four to eight colleagues – white men, white women, and men and women of color. Intact work groups, management teams, or diversity councils are good groups with whom to do this activity.

1] Think of an organization of which you are all a part.

_____

_____

_____

_____

2] Have each team member list the unspoken "rules of the road" that define how one contributes and operates successfully within the organization.

_____

_____

_____

_____

_____

3] List everyone's rules on a master list. Discuss the rules only enough to get clarification. It is not necessary that everyone in the group agree on every rule. Condense or combine any rules on the list, if possible.

_____

_____

_____

_____

4] Once the full list is created, give each person three votes for each of the questions below (use three sticky dots of one color and three sticky dots of another color). Ask each team member to place the dots on the page to rank the full list the following ways:

a. Three most influential rules that impact people's behavior in the organization (using dots of one color)

_____

_____

_____

_____

_____

b. Three least influential rules that impact people's behavior in the organization (using dots of another color)

_____

_____

_____

_____

_____

5] Tally the votes and designate the group's top three for each category.

_____

_____

_____

_____

_____

6] Share insights and observations from the tally results.

_____

_____

_____

_____

_____

7] Optional discussion questions:

a. How do the rules of the road impact people's behavior in the organization?

_____

_____

_____

_____

_____

b. How do these behaviors differ? What factors determine who behaves in what way in response to the rule?

_____

_____

_____

_____

_____

c. What are the costs to people and the organization when many of these rules are unconscious or invisible?

_____

_____

_____

_____

_____

d. What are the informal and formal ways people are taught the rules of the road?

_____

_____

_____

_____

_____

_____

MISTAKE OF THE MONTH CLUB

GOALS:
To better differentiate between mistakes you and others can learn from and inexcusable faux pas.

To model vulnerability.

To practice diversity partnership skills by being able to be "raggedy" (more honest and willing to make mistakes with the intent of learning) with/from each other.
Estimated Time: One 60- to 90-minute meeting a month plus personal time during the month to take notes. This requires an ongoing commitment of at least three to six months.

STEPS
1] Select two or three colleagues with whom you have an honest and open working relationship. Look for people who have demonstrated that they value giving and receiving feedback to/from one another.

2] Agree to meet together once a month for a 60- to 90-minute period. Doing lunch together might work well.

3] During the month, pay attention to missteps you make that lead to deeper understanding or partnership. Look for situations when you or another person makes a mistake about a diversity-related issue.

4] Keep written notes over the month about the following:
a. What difficult conversations did you witness or have with your colleague, and how did he/she or you resolve or not resolve the dilemma?

_____

_____

_____

_____

_____

_____

_____

_____

b. What skills did you or others use that aided resolution?

_____

_____

_____

_____

_____

_____

_____

_____

_____

_____

_____

_____

_____

_____

c. What actions and behaviors did you observe that escalated the conflict?

_____

_____

_____

_____

_____

_____

_____

_____

_____

_____

_____

_____

_____

d. What did you learn from the mistake or misstep, and how did or might you apply
    the learning to negotiating/strengthening diversity partnerships?

_____

_____

_____

_____

_____

_____

_____

_____

_____

_____

5] During your monthly meeting, plan time to hear from each person about their
    mistake and what they learned. Share your best mistake and what makes it so.
    The other group members will act as consultants to assist each person with
    answering the following:

a. What are the key learnings that have future application in developing diversity
    partnerships and impacting business results positively?

_____

_____

_____

_____

_____

_____

_____

_____

_____

_____

b. What do your colleagues know now that they didn't know before they made
the mistake?

_____

_____

_____

_____

_____

_____

_____

_____

c. What insight might exist, but is not readily seen by the person who is sharing
the mistake?

_____

_____

_____

_____

_____

_____

_____

_____

6] As a full group, discuss what patterns you notice in the mistakes that are brought
to the table. In the coming month, invite people to notice some invisible areas that
can challenge them to examine an unseen angle in their own diversity partnership
interactions. Help each other discover what each person doesn't know or see in
their attempts at partnership. Talk about the costs to the business and your individual
and collective goals when partnerships are not examined and reenergized.

APPENDICES

KEY CONCEPTS

European-American or American White Male Culture

Culture describes shared values and beliefs of a group. U.S. American white male culture is interesting in that it can be seen and described by those who are not members of the culture, yet for many white men the characteristics they share with other white men are most often invisible. This stems in part from the fact that most white men rarely have to step out of their culture, while many white women and people of color learn to be bi-cultural, often moving in and out of white male culture on a daily basis. The paradox is that in order for one to best understand one's culture, one has to leave it.

The shared characteristics of white men in the United States determine, in large part, how things get done and the norms of interaction, both business and personal. Within a culture, individuals will vary in their knowledge, acceptance and support of the culture. Some won't know they are members of a group with a distinct culture. There are six themes of the U.S. white male culture we engage in our work:

- Rugged individualism
- Low tolerance for uncertainty and ambiguity
- Focus on action over reflection (doing over being)
- Rationality over emotion (head over heart)
- Time as linear and future focused
- Status and rank over connection

The cultural literature often refers to the above characteristics as "American Culture" while at the same time identifying African American, Asian American and other ethnic subcultures of the U.S. as something else. The white male facet of what is simply described as American Culture often goes unspoken and remains invisible.

Since most organizations and institutions in the U.S. are based on white male cultural values such as those listed above, all of us — white men, white women, and people of color — have learned to operate in this culture.

A brief note about the words we use. Technically speaking the term European-American refers more to ethnicity and region of origin, while the terms white and male refer more to race and gender, respectively. We have chosen to describe the above culture more often as white male culture in the U.S. in part because we have found many white men tend to more easily identify themselves as white male than European-American. Please use the term you most prefer.

Partnership and Partnership Culture

Partner: A person associated with another or member of a business partnership.

Have you ever felt like a child at work? Have you ever wondered why your manager thought you needed to be protected from what everyone knew was coming (downsizing, a merger, plant closings, a new CEO, etc.)? When you have that feeling or are asking similar questions, you are probably responding to the parental nature of organizations. Most organizations are hierarchical and depend on predictability, and command and control, to meet business goals. Another way to think about the parental nature of organizations is to view them as patriarchal – or "father knows best." Patriarchy is different than building a diversity partnership culture in our organizations. Peter Block dedicates Chapter Two of his 1993 book, *Stewardship*, to partnership as an alternative to patriarchy. We believe that diversity partnerships are on the cutting edge of changing organizations. Block describes partnership as having four requirements that need to be demonstrated for real partnership to develop. His requirements fit the intention of White Men As Full Diversity Partners®' diversity partnership work.

Block's four requirements for real partnership include:
- Exchange of purpose – "Purpose gets defined through dialogue." (Block, 1993 p. 29)
- Right to say no – "If we cannot say no, then saying yes has no meaning." (p. 30)
- Joint accountability – Each person is responsible for outcomes and the current situation. "If people in organizations want the freedom partnership offers, the price of that freedom is to take personal accountability for the success and failure of our unit and our community." (p. 30)
- Absolute honesty – It's essential for partnership. (p. 30)

Crutch-Free Diversity Partnership Framework

- Our respective roles are clear and we understand them rather than assuming what we each mean. I ask before assuming I know.

- We agree on how we will engage conflict.

- We actively apply and live in the key paradoxes. Individually, we take time to find out whether our perspectives match, or not. We look at how each of us uses the paradoxes – how we demonstrate them in our behavior.

- We use frequent direct feedback about what works in the partnership and what doesn't work. We listen to understand. We talk about how the contributions we make to our partnership affect our commitment to our work and each other.

- We acknowledge the steps we've taken to support and challenge each other. We recognize that our diversity partners may have very different views and understandings of the issues we are facing together. We acknowledge that our frames of reference have been affected by differences of gender, race, class, sexual orientation, experience, etc. It's our job to understand each other's world views and their influence on how we work together.

- We show respect for each other in the moment…when it counts. Some of these moments will occur when our partner is not present. These will be opportunities we can use to demonstrate respect for our partner and our partnership.

- We attend to a broken trust between us, rather than assume that our partnership is a lost cause. "Once broken, never regained," is unacceptable as our first response. Tears in the fabric of our partnership are used to test our commitment, demonstrate tenacity and build skill. We refuse to hold on to misunderstandings. We do that by scheduling time to air and resolve misunderstandings.

Paradox

The American Heritage Dictionary of the English Language defines paradox as a seemingly contradictory statement that may nonetheless be true. Another of its definitions suggests that paradox can and does live in an individual, group, situation or action that exhibits inexplicable or contradictory aspects.

Contradictions often contain conflict, particularly when the contradictions co-exist at the same time in the same individual, group and/or situation. Diversity partnership is a hotbed of paradox. We offer four that show up repeatedly in diversity partnership work that require conscious attention and skill building. Diversity partners build skill at living with paradox and conflict. Kenwyn K. Smith and David N. Berg describe paradox in detail in their book, *Paradoxes of Group Life*.

Paradox #1 – Individual/Group:
White men are *both* individuals *and* members of the white male group. When white men acknowledge their membership in the white male group, they do not give up their individuality.

Example:
"Don't lump me in with other white guys. Maybe I'm different."
"I've never thought of myself as being a member of a white male group, and I am."

Paradox *Continued*

Paradox #2 – Difference/Sameness

A deeper picture of diversity requires both a focus on difference *and* sameness, diversity *and* commonality. Each can only be defined in terms of the other. For example, being color-conscious *and* color-blind simultaneously.

Example:
"I treat everyone the same. I don't see color."
"I want my coworkers to see my color. It's an important part of me."

Paradox #3 – Support/Challenge

Breakthrough learning is created by diversity partners who support *and* challenge each other. Partners do not choose one or the other side of this or any paradox. Both sides are necessary in effective results-focused diversity partnerships.

Example:
"We need to be patient and understanding here…let people come along at their own pace."
"That behavior is wrong and it must change."

Paradox #4 – No Fault/Responsibility:

It is not my fault *and* I am responsible. Often white men feel they are being asked to carry the personal burden of the historical mistreatment of other groups. It is not our fault and we are vital parts of the dialogue needed to create more equitable systems for everyone, including white men.

Example:
"I didn't create this situation…and I can and will look at my responsibility for keeping it in place."

Difficult Conversations

A difficult conversation is any conversation you find hard to initiate, participate in and complete. Difficult conversations require preparation. The ability to engage in difficult conversations is a key concept of diversity partnership work.*

Difficult conversations have three parts:

1. **Content:** What is it you want to talk about? What are your intentions for discussing it?

2. **Feelings:** What are you feeling as you prepare for the conversation? It does little good to attempt to hide or bury your feelings.

3. **The identity conversation:** How does this situation threaten our sense of who we are?

Preparation:

- Uncover your assumptions and *intentions* before you schedule time for the conversation.

- Don't assume you know your partner's intentions. You don't.

- Difficult conversations require risk-taking; take some.

*This material has been adapted from the book *Difficult Conversations*.

GLOSSARY

Systemic Privilege/Advantage
Systemic privilege is the unspoken and unacknowledged benefits that come to a person through no virtue of their own but are made to look normal and available to any person who wants them. These benefits are often invisible to those who receive them and clearly visible to those who don't.

Classism
Classism is prejudice and/or discrimination, either personal or institutional, against people because of their real or perceived economic status or background. *(http://cluh2.tripod.com/definitions.html#classism)*

Collusion
Collusion is the often unconscious actions that reinforce/support the status quo that benefit some at the expense of others. Collusion can be conscious or unconscious, active or passive.

Heterosexism
Heterosexism is action taken to limit people's rights and privileges or access to them, based on the conscious or unconscious belief or opinion that heterosexuality is the normal and right expression of sexuality and any other expression is abnormal and wrong. The privileges and rights that are denied can be legislative, public and familial.

Fluid Identity
Fluid Identity is the concept that identity is not rigid but can and does change. This idea is often used in terms of gender, sexuality, and race, as well as other factors of identity. This concept is fundamentally contrary to binary systems. A person who feels her/his identity is fluid often believes that rigid categories are oppressive and incapable of accurately describing her/his experience and identities. *(http://cluh2.tripod.com/)*

Homophobia
Homophobia is the fear or hatred of gays, lesbians, or queer-identified people in general. It can be manifested as an intense dislike or rejection of such people, or violent actions against them. *(http://cluh2.tripod.com/definitions.html)*
See the definition of Heterosexism, above.

Sex Reassignment Surgery (SRS)

SRS is the surgical procedure to modify one's primary sexual characteristics (genitalia) from those of one sex to those of the opposite sex. SRS may also include secondary surgery such as breast augmentation or reduction and/or removing the Adam's apple. *(http://www.tg2tg.org/forums/lifestyles)*

SOFFA

A SOFFA is a Significant Other, Friend, Family, or Ally of a transsexual, transgender, inter-sex or other gender-variant person. *(http://www.virtualcity.com/)*

Transgender (TG)

Transgender is a more recently adopted umbrella term that includes all persons who engage in cross-gender activities or lifestyles regardless of motivation or sexual orientation. *(http://www.tg2tg.org/forums/lifestyles)*

Transsexual* (TS)

Transsexual describes an individual whose gender identity is the opposite of his or her physical sex. Typically such individuals desire modification of their physical body (i.e., SRS) to match their gender identity, and derive no "thrill," erotic or otherwise, from merely wearing the clothing associated with the opposite biological gender. *(http://www.tg2tg.org/forums/lifestyles)*

* Transsexual may also be spelled transexual, depending on country of origin. *(http://pages.sbcglobal.net/texasrat/page9.html)*

White Guilt

White guilt is a frequent response of white people to learning about white privilege. White guilt makes white individuals feel shameful about the history of oppression of people of color and the role white persons have played in perpetuating that system, as well as their individual complicity with that system. *(http://cluh2.tripod.com/definitions.html)*

SUGGESTED READING:

Arrien, Angeles. *The Four-Fold Way: Walking the Paths of the Warrior, Teacher, Healer, and Visionary.* HarperSanFrancisco: 1993. ISBN: 0-06-250059-7

Bilodeau, M.S., Lorrainne. *The Anger Workbook.* MIF Books: 1992. ISBN: 1-56731-202-0

Block, Peter. *Stewardship.* Berrett Koehler: 1993. ISBN: 1-881052-28-1

Bridges, William. *Managing Transitions, Making The Most of Change.* Addison Wesley: 1991. ISBN: 0-201-55073-3

Cashman, Kevin. *Leadership from the Inside Out.* Executive Excellence Publishing: 1998. ISBN: 1-890009-29-6

Dana, Daniel, Ph.D, *Managing Differences: How to Build Better Relationships at Work and Home.* MTI Publications: 1997. ISBN: 0-9621534-3-5

Goleman, Daniel, Richard Boyatzis, and Annie McKee. *Primal Leadership: Realizing The Power Of Emotional Intelligence.* Harvard Business School Press: 2002. ISBN:1-57851-486-X

Johnson, Barry. *Polarity Management: Identifying and Managing Unsolvable Problems.* Human Resource Development Press: 1992. ISBN: 0-87425-176-1

Lukeman, Alex and Gayle. *Beyond Blame: Reclaiming The Power You Give To Others.* North Star Publications: 1997. ISBN: 1-880823-14-4

Maurer, Rick. *Feedback Toolkit: 16 Tools for Better Communication in the Workplace.* Productivity Press: 1994. ISBN:1-56327-056-0

McGraw, Phillip C., Ph.D. *Life Strategies: Doing What Works, Doing What Matters.* Hyperion: 1999. ISBN: 0-7868-8459-2

Pfeffer, Jeffrey. *Managing with Power: Politics and Influence in Organizations.* Harvard Business School Press: 1992. ISBN: 0-87584-314-X

Scott, Susan. *Fierce Conversations: Achieving Success at Work & in Life, One Conversation at a Time.* Berkley Books: 2002. ISBN: 0-425-19337-3

Stone, Douglas, Bruce Patton and Sheila Heen. *Difficult Conversations: How to Discuss What Matters Most.* Penguin Books: 2000. ISBN: 0-14-028852 X

Takaki, Ronald. *From Different Shores: Perspectives on Race and Ethnicity in America.* Second Edition. Oxford University Press: 1994. ISBN: 0-19-508368-7

Takaki, Ronald. *A Different Mirror: A History of Multicultural America,* 1993. ISBN: 0-316-83111-5

Wheatley, Margaret, J. *Leadership and the New Science: Discovering Order in a Chaotic World.* Berrett-Koehler Publishers: 1999. ISBN: 1-57675-055-8

Whyte, David. *The Heart Aroused: Poetry and the Preservation of the Soul in Corporate America.* Revised Edition. Doubleday: 2002. ISBN 0-385-48418-6

Wylie, Pete, Dr., and Dr. Mardy Grothe. *Can This Partnership Be Saved? Improving (or Salvaging) Your Key Business Relationships.* Upstart Publishing Company, Inc.: 1993. ISBN: 0-936894-42-3

www.wmfdp.com
See the Online Resources page.

Diversity Partnership Tips for White Women and People of Color to Engage White Men: A Skills Building Field Guide

By Jo Ann Morris, Bill Proudman, Michael Welp

Open this book, open your mind, and climb out of your box. This field guide tackles workplace diversity with startling candor and delivers refreshingly practical solutions for individuals and groups. You'll encounter provocative questions that stretch your thinking and lead to surprising new insights about the assumptions that drive your behavior. For instance, did you know that your ability to fully partner with others is often blocked not by their resistance, but by your own hidden beliefs? Before you can cultivate truly effective partnerships, there is some essential groundwork you must do on your own. This guide will show you how to move from low collaboration to high collaboration. Of course, the other part of the equation is understanding others. In this book you'll learn about the unconscious attitudes that govern the ways white men do – and don't – participate in diversity efforts. You'll even discover why it's difficult for white women and people of color to see what white men really know about diversity. (Hint: white men are people, too.) Consider this guide required reading for all white women and people of color who want to work more effectively with white men and others.

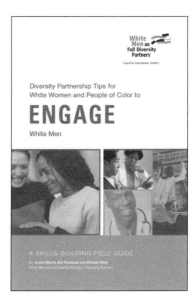

$15.95 ISBN 0-9754192-2-6

order books at www.wmfdp.com

Eight Critical Leadership Skills Created Through Effective Diversity Partnerships: A Skills Building Field Guide

By Michael Welp, Jo Ann Morris, Bill Proudman

The secret is out: While there's no shortage of business leadership programs to sign up for, they may not be the best places to build the complex skills you need to effectively lead in today's complex workplaces. This landmark field guide brings the most sought-after talents right to your doorstep. You'll learn how real leadership is best cultivated: by working with the diverse people around you. As you read and reflect on the thought-provoking questions and do the activities described, you'll boost your ability to lead – and improve your organization's business results.

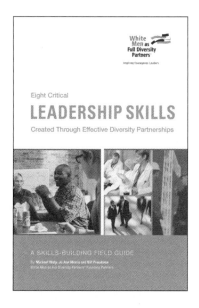

We consider such defining questions as: What is courage? Where does it come from? And why do you need it at work? You'll find out how to escape the all-too-common trap of simplistic either/or thinking and embrace the normal para-doxes of every workplace – so you can work with reality instead of against it. Using our roadmap for difficult conversations, you'll learn about the detours, dangers and delays you're likely to encounter so you can anticipate and overcome them. In the same vein, we show you how to stay on your intended path through periods of change by allowing for the inevitable turbulence, uncer-tainty and resistance. And, not least, we explore how you can develop a fuller and deeper kind of leadership by connecting your head and your heart.

$15.95 ISBN 0-9754192-0-X

order books at www.wmfdp.com

AUTHOR BIOGRAPHIES

BILL PROUDMAN is a founding partner of White Men as Full Diversity Partners®, a consulting firm that develops courageous leaders who build effective partnerships between white men, white women, and men and women of color in organizations. He pioneered white-male-only learning labs in the mid-90s after noticing that white male leaders repeatedly disengaged from diversity efforts, almost always looking to white women, and men and women of color, to lead and educate. This provocative work became the seed for his involvement in the creation of WMFDP.

Bill remains an avid diversity learner and an impassioned believer that everyone has a role to play to create just and equitable communities and organizations. He has 25 years experience as a process facilitator and consultant working on the human side of organizational change and transformation. Bill has been an ongoing consultant to the American Leadership Forum having designed and conducted numerous residential leadership development programs since the early 90s. *Bill splits time between homes in Portland, Oregon and the southern Cascades of Washington State. He can be reached at 503-281-5585 or proudman@wmfdp.com.*

MICHAEL WELP, PH.D. is a founding partner of White Men as Full Diversity Partners®. Known for his authentic, trust-building style, Michael works to develop leadership in everyone. Michael has facilitated interracial teambuilding for South African corporations, and has authored a dissertation and book chapter about white men and diversity. An adjunct faculty at the Capella University, he is the recipient of the Minnesota Organization Development Practitioner of the Year Award and is a professional member of NTL Institute for Applied Behavioral Science. Michael also founded EqualVoice, an organization development consulting firm known for building collaborative work cultures and for its transformative approaches to conflict. *He lives in Sandpoint, Idaho and can be reached at 208.263.6775 or welp@wmfdp.com.*

JO ANN MORRIS is a founding partner of White Men as Full Diversity Partners®. She is an executive coach and organization change consultant. Her practice is noted for its Integral Coaching methods for executives and Diversity In-depth Coaching.

Jo Ann was an Information Technology and Programming Manager for 15 years prior to WMFDP. Jo Ann's most challenging technology position was with Fidelity Mutual funds. She was their software programming manager.

She has been a guest lecturer at the Lyndon Baines Johnson Public Executive Institute at the University of Texas at Austin and at the Brandeis University Women in Management Program. She has designed and facilitated diversity initiatives with clients ranging from The Greater Greensboro North Carolina Chamber of Commerce, Exxon Chemicals and Lucent Technologies to the General Services Administration and American Express. *She lives in Connecticut and can be reached at 202.352.4776 or morris@wmfdp.com.*

ABOUT WMFDP

White Men as Full Diversity Partners® is a culture-change consulting firm. We offer coaching, curriculum design, learning lab intensives and system-wide change opportunities to inspire organizational leadership to make commitments, and to operate with courage when addressing issues related to inclusion and diversity. The leading edge of diversity work involves white men, white women and people of color, partnering with each other to move white men from the sidelines of diversity efforts – to being fully in the midst of these efforts at all levels of the organization. In the end we do three things: build skills, transform mindsets, and create powerful partnerships within the organizations we serve. Visit our website for more about WMFDP.

www.wmfdp.com